BIOGRAPHIES

THOMAS JEFFERSON

by Laura K. Murray

PEBBLE
a capstone imprint

Pebble Explore is published by Pebble, an imprint of Capstone.
1710 Roe Crest Drive
North Mankato, Minnesota 56003
www.capstonepub.com

Library of Congress Cataloging-in-Publication data is available on the Library of Congress website.
ISBN: 978-1-9771-1363-4 (library binding)
ISBN: 978-1-9771-1807-3 (paperback)
ISBN: 978-1-9771-1371-9 (eBook PDF)

Summary: Explores the life, challenges, and accomplishments of Thomas Jefferson, the third president of the United States.

Image Credits
Alamy: ClassicStock, 12; Granger: Sarin Images, 16; Library of Congress: 15; National Gallery of Art: Gift of Thomas Jefferson Coolidge IV in memory of his great-grandfather, Thomas Jefferson Coolidge, his grandfather, Thomas Jefferson Coolidge II, and his father, Thomas Jefferson Coolidge III, 5, 29; Newscom: akg-images, 11, Design Pics, 9, Picture History, 17, 20; Shutterstock: Everett Historical, 19, Jess Kraft, 24, Joseph Sohm, 21, kapooklook01 (geometric background), cover, back cover, 2, 29, N8Allen, 25, Tony Baggett, 26 (bottom); SuperStock: 4X5 Collection, cover, 1, 27; Svetlana Zhurkin: 26 (top); The New York Public Library: 7, 23; Wikimedia: William Morris, 18

Editorial Credits
Christopher Harbo, editor; Elyse White, designer; Jo Miller and Svetlana Zhurkin, media researchers; Katy LaVigne, production specialist

All internet sites appearing in back matter were available and accurate when this book was sent to press.

Printed and bound in China.
2489

Table of Contents

Words in **bold** are in the glossary.

Who Was Thomas Jefferson?

Thomas Jefferson helped form the United States of America. He was the main writer of the **Declaration of Independence**. Later Thomas became the third **president** of the United States.

Thomas wanted the world to look up to the United States. He made the country bigger and stronger. He also never stopped learning and teaching others. His words and ideas will be remembered forever.

5

Growing Up Thomas

Thomas was born nearly 300 years ago on April 13, 1743. His family lived in Shadwell, Virginia. At that time, Virginia was one of 13 **colonies** owned by Great Britain. Thomas had 10 brothers and sisters. His family owned large farms. They had **enslaved** people to do the work on these farms.

As a child, Thomas liked to read and explore outside. Thomas began school at age 5. He learned history, science, and other languages.

A mill on the Jefferson family's farm in Shadwell, Virginia

When he was 17, Thomas went to the College of William and Mary in Virginia. He studied law and became a good writer. After school, Thomas became a **lawyer**.

In 1769, Thomas began working in Virginia's **government**. At this time, Virginia and the other colonies were owned by Great Britain. But Thomas and other people in the colonies wanted to be free of Great Britain. They felt that British laws were unfair. Thomas wrote about why the colonies should be free.

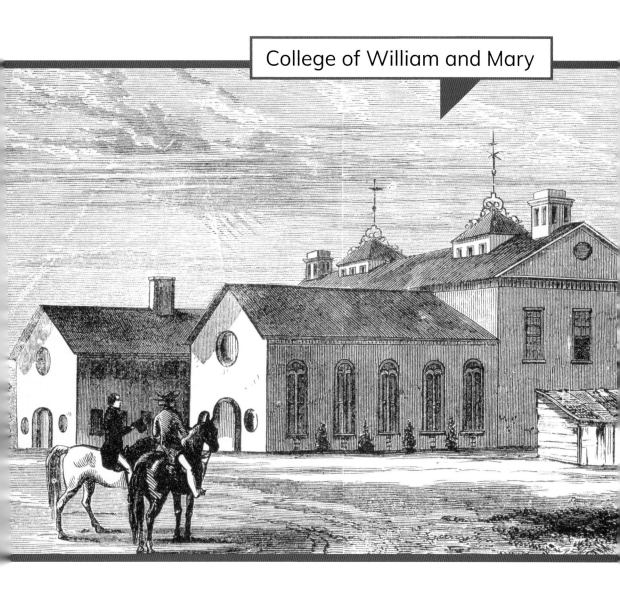

College of William and Mary

Home and Family

In 1768, Thomas began building a house. It sat on a hill near the place he grew up. He named the house Monticello. It meant "little mountain" in Italian.

Thomas started building his home when he was 25 years old. Enslaved people were made to do a lot of the work. Monticello took almost 40 years to finish. At the end, it had 43 rooms. The land around it also had gardens and other buildings.

Monticello

Thomas and his wife, Martha

Thomas married Martha Wayles Skelton in 1772 at age 28. They had six children. Only two of them lived to be adults. They were named Martha and Mary. In 1782, Thomas's wife Martha died. Thomas did not marry again.

Thomas had many hobbies. He liked to learn about music, plants, math, and art. He played the violin and rode horses. He also loved books. His library at Monticello had thousands of books.

Words for a New Country

In 1776, the colonies wanted to break away from Great Britain. Thomas and four other men were asked to write the Declaration of Independence. Thomas wrote the first draft. The **document** told everyone that the colonies were now free from Great Britain.

The Declaration of Independence became official on July 4, 1776. The date became the birthday for the new country. But the colonies still had to fight for freedom from Great Britain in the **Revolutionary War** (1775-1783).

Thomas (right) wrote the Declaration of Independence with Benjamin Franklin (left) and John Adams (center).

Thomas stayed busy during and after the war. He led Virginia as **governor** from 1779 to 1781. Then he worked for the United States in France. He became the first secretary of state in 1790. He helped the United States work with other countries.

Thomas (left) as secretary of state

Thomas as president

Thomas ran for president in 1796. He lost, but became vice president under John Adams. In 1800, Thomas ran for president again. He won and became the third U.S. president in 1801.

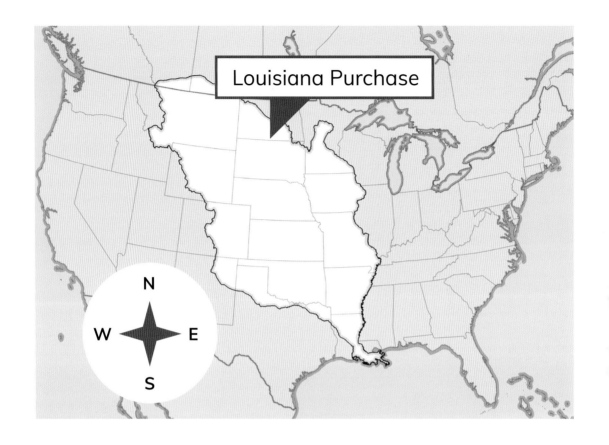

Louisiana Purchase

As president, Thomas made the United States bigger. In 1803, he bought land west of the Mississippi River from France. This deal nearly doubled the size of the country! It became known as the Louisiana Purchase.

Thomas wanted to learn about the new land. He hired Meriwether Lewis and William Clark to explore and make maps. A young American Indian woman named Sacagawea guided them.

Lewis and Clark with Sacagawea and her husband behind them

Later Years

In 1804, Thomas ran for president again and won. Four years later, he moved back to Monticello. In 1815, Thomas sold more than 6,000 of his books to the government. The books helped start a new Library of Congress. It is the main library of the United States.

Thomas's books

University of Virginia

Thomas helped start the University of Virginia. The school opened in 1825. Thomas was proud of his work. He was called the father of the school.

Thomas kept writing as he got older. He wrote letters to people around the world to share ideas. He and his friend John Adams often wrote to each other. At age 77, Thomas began writing a book about his own life.

Thomas died on July 4, 1826, at Monticello. He was 83 years old. It was America's 50th birthday. His friend John Adams died just a few hours later.

Remembering Jefferson

Today people can visit places to learn about Thomas's life. The Jefferson **Memorial** is in Washington, D.C. A statue of Thomas stands inside the building. In South Dakota, Thomas's face is carved into Mount Rushmore.

Mount Rushmore

Thomas Jefferson

Monticello

More than 400,000 people go see Monticello each year. They walk through the house and gardens. They can see Thomas's grave too. On Thomas's birthday, people give speeches and play music at Monticello.

People remember Thomas in other ways. They see his face on the $2 bill and the nickel. They also read his words in the Declaration of Independence. His words are still powerful today. Every 4th of July, people celebrate the birth of the United States.

Thomas Jefferson was an important leader in American history. As president, he helped the United States grow. His ideas about freedom helped make America the country we know today.

Important Dates

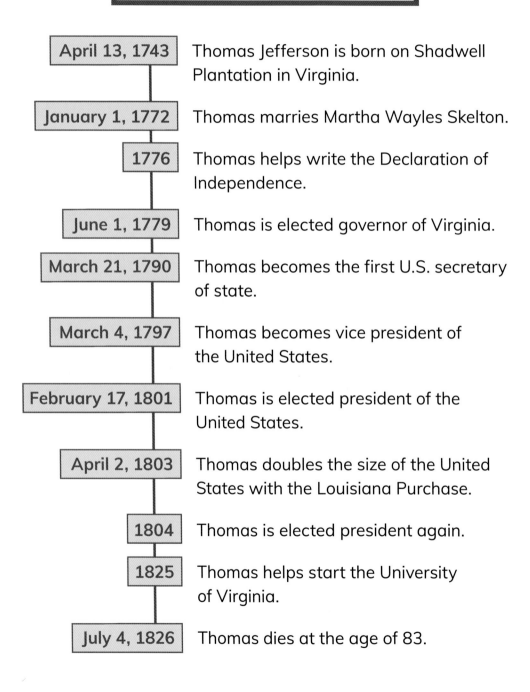

April 13, 1743	Thomas Jefferson is born on Shadwell Plantation in Virginia.
January 1, 1772	Thomas marries Martha Wayles Skelton.
1776	Thomas helps write the Declaration of Independence.
June 1, 1779	Thomas is elected governor of Virginia.
March 21, 1790	Thomas becomes the first U.S. secretary of state.
March 4, 1797	Thomas becomes vice president of the United States.
February 17, 1801	Thomas is elected president of the United States.
April 2, 1803	Thomas doubles the size of the United States with the Louisiana Purchase.
1804	Thomas is elected president again.
1825	Thomas helps start the University of Virginia.
July 4, 1826	Thomas dies at the age of 83.

Fast Facts

Name:
Thomas Jefferson

Role:
Third president of the United States

Life dates:
April 13, 1743 to July 4, 1826

Key accomplishments:
Thomas Jefferson served as the main writer of the Declaration of Independence. He also served as the first U.S. secretary of state. In 1801, Thomas became the third president of the United States. During his time in office, he made a deal with France called the Louisiana Purchase. It doubled the size of the United States.

Glossary

colony (KAH-luh-nee)—an area that has been settled by people from another country

Declaration of Independence (dek-luh-RAY-shuhn UV in-di-PEN-duhnss)—a document that declares the United States a free country

document (DAHK-yuh-muhnt)—a piece of writing that contains important information

enslave (en-SLAYV)—to make someone lose their freedom

government (GUHV-urn-muhnt)—the group of people who make laws and decisions for a group

governor (GUHV-urn-ur)—the leader of a state

lawyer (LOI-ur)—a person who is trained to advise people about the law

memorial (muh-MOR-ee-uhl)—something that is built or done to help people remember a person or event

president (PREZ-uh-duhnt)—the highest elected job in a class, business, or country

Revolutionary War (rev-uh-LOO-shuhn-air-ee WOR)—the American colonies' fight from 1775 to 1783 for freedom from Great Britain

Read More

Chang, Kirsten. *Mount Rushmore*. Minneapolis: Bellwether Media, 2019.

Clay, Kathryn. *The Declaration of Independence: Introducing Primary Sources*. North Mankato, MN: Capstone, 2018.

O'Donoghue, Sean. *Thomas Jefferson and the Louisiana Purchase*. New York: PowerKids Press, 2017.

Internet Sites

Declaration of Independence
https://www.archives.gov/founding-docs/declaration

John Adams and Thomas Jefferson
https://www.pbs.org/ktca/liberty/popup_adams-jefferson.html

Monticello
https://home.monticello.org/

Index